MW01152186

anderson & roe
DUOS DUETS

Tambourin Chinois
(Chinese Drum)

Fritz Kreisler
Arranged by Greg Anderson

I don't mind telling you that I enjoyed very much writing my Tambourin Chinois. The idea for it came to me after a visit to the Chinese theater in San Francisco—not that the music there suggested any theme, but it gave me the impulse to write a free fantasy in the Chinese manner.[1]

—Fritz Kreisler

Foreword

Regarded as one of the greatest violinists of all time, Fritz Kreisler composed dozens of short works for violin and piano to perform on his recitals. Many of these musical delicatessens evoke sentiment for the cozy lifestyles of pre-war Vienna; others venture to imitate the style of composers such as Gaetano Pugnani, Giuseppe Tartini, and Antonio Vivaldi.

Audiences of the day likely heard *Tambourin Chinois*, composed in 1910, as avant-garde new music by a composer experimenting with exotic musical forms. But other than its use of the pentatonic scale or occasional parallel fifths, *Tambourin Chinois* has little to do with actual Chinese music—not surprising, considering Kreisler had such limited exposure to genuine examples of the country's culture and traditions. In the end, the cultural authenticity is beside the point; the piece is a joyous and delightful musical gem, a celebration of imagined worlds and faraway lands, and a reminder that we all perceive differently the world around us.

Similarly, I make no pretense to faithfully recapture the exactitudes of the original in this arrangement for piano duet; it represents my reaction to Kreisler's *Tambourin Chinois*. I've replaced the excitement of violinists' wildfire tempos with increased complexity (but slower pace) as the pianists exchange in a musical—and physical—banter. One of my more acrobatic arrangements, the pianists are asked to recreate the playfulness of the music through dance-like interaction. It is my hope that, while learning the piece, the struggles of coordination will lead to fits of laughter—as opposed to feelings of malice! For the most part, play the music non-legato and the accompanimental textures with a quiet, inner energy. A jauntier pulse is recommended, fused with endless flair, gusto, and contagious spirit.

I am deeply appreciative of Elizabeth Joy Roe and Kim Craig for their generous support and editorial considerations in the preparation of this arrangement.

—Greg Anderson

[1] Frederick H. Martens, *Violin Mastery: Talks with Master Violinists and Teachers* (New York: Frederick A. Stokes Company, 1919), 108.

Alfred Music Publishing Co., Inc.
P.O. Box 10003
Van Nuys, CA 91410-0003
alfred.com

ISBN-10: 0-7390-9298-7
ISBN-13: 978-0-7390-9298-9

Cover photo
Chinese dragon: © Shutterstock.com / Momo0607

for Kim Craig

Tambourin Chinois
(Chinese Drum)

Fritz Kreisler (1875–1962)
Op. 3
Arr. Greg Anderson

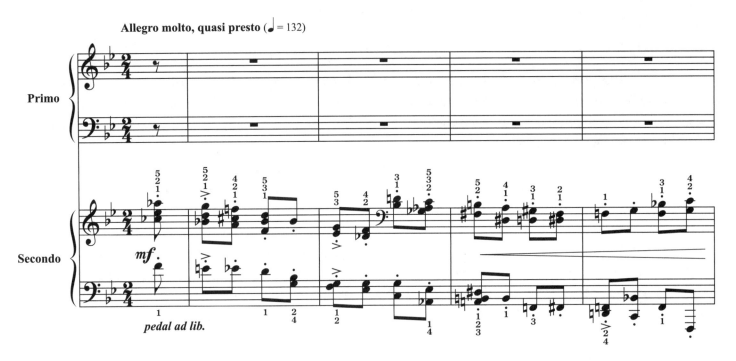

a For passages marked **over**, play *above* the other performer's hand—near the fallboard with wrist elevated.
For passages marked **under**, play *below* the other performer's hand—with wrist lowered.

5

(b) The glissandi should begin slowly and gradually accelerate into a playful descent of noise. The glissandi need not conclude on any particular pitch.

© Release the RH D immediately to allow for *primo*.

(e) Play RH over *primo's* right arm and then quickly return to play the next measure.

(f) To compensate for the awkward angle of the left arm during the crossovers, these notes can be played more comfortably without the thumb.

(g) The players' arms are interwoven. In measures 168–180, *secondo* plays RH over *primo's* left arm and under *primo's* right arm.

14

(h) Stand to reach the notes in measures 180–181 and then gradually sit while playing the scale in measures 182–185.

(i) Play both hands under *secondo's* arms as *secondo* stands to reach the notes in measures 180–181.

ⓙ Finish RH glissando over *primo's* left arm.